Grant Wood's renowned painting *American Gothic* is known throughout the world. The image of a farm woman and man standing with a pitchfork in front of their farmhouse has become an American icon instantly recognizable around the globe. But who is the artist behind the painting?

Unlike his contemporaries, Grant Wood painted simple paintings with a classical feel. He chose to paint the people and places around him, and this new style of art—known as Regionalism—changed the way people looked at the world around them.

Lively and informative, this is the first biography of Grant Wood published specifically for young readers. The engaging text and stunning reproductions of Grant Wood's artwork combine to create an inspiring story of a determined artist that is perfect for both home and classroom libraries.

"The author writes with great skill, telling Wood's story not simply with dates and places, but with anecdotes, descriptions, and snatches of conversation."
—*School L*

South
Dakota

Minnesota

Wisconsin

Mississippi River

IOWA

Stone City • • Anamosa

Cedar Rapids ●

Iowa City ●

Nebraska

Illinois

Missouri

Kansas

Artist in Overalls

The Life of Grant Wood

Artist in Overalls

The Life of Grant Wood

John Duggleby

chronicle books

San Francisco

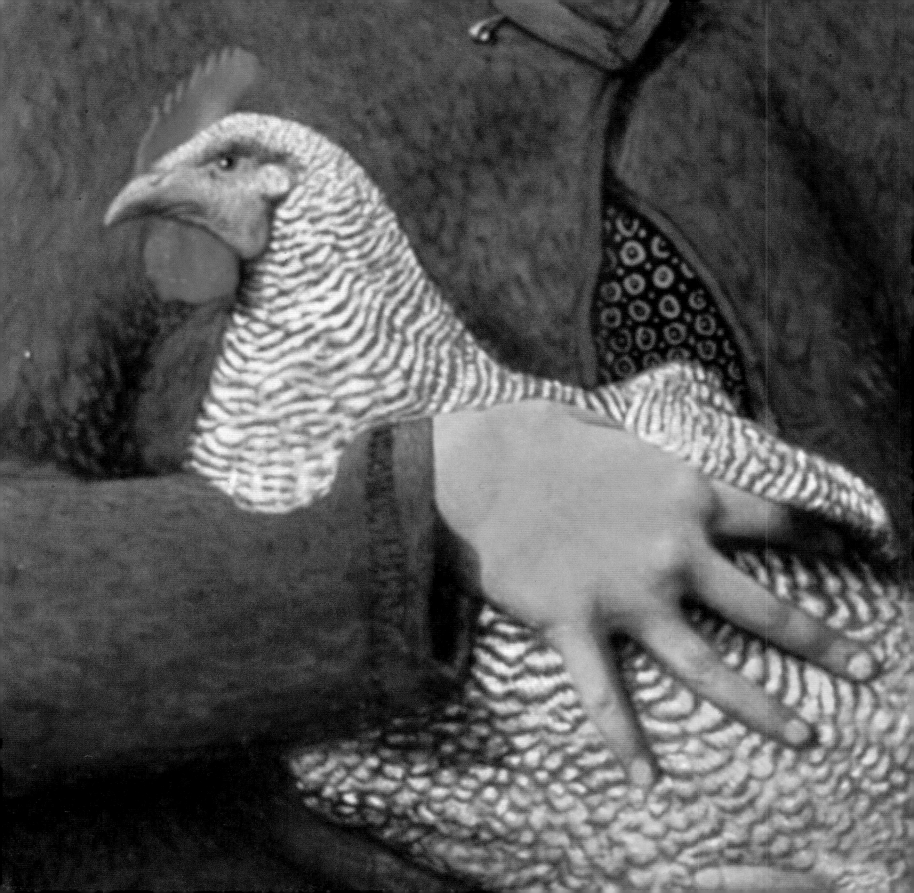

— CHAPTER ONE —

Life on the Farm

When Grant Wood was born, in 1891, America was going through a great change called the Industrial Revolution. People were moving by the millions from farms to cities, looking for jobs in factories and shops.

Grant's parents were different. They owned a small farm in Iowa, and they were determined to stay there. The Woods grew up in the country, and they wanted their children to as well.

Grant was a shy boy. More than anything else, he liked to draw. He drew whenever he could, using charred black sticks pulled carefully from the cooking stove and white cardboard torn from cracker boxes. That was all he had. In 1898 fancy drawing supplies were only a dream for a farm boy whose house didn't even have electricity.

Everything Grant saw around him ended up on those cracker boxes. He drew houses, barns, trees, cows, cats—but most of all, he drew chickens. They were like pets to him, the way they pecked at the cookies he shared as he sat outside his house. His favorites were his mother's Plymouth Rock hens, with their black and white feathers arranged in neat crescent-moon shapes. He drew them every way possible—sitting on giant piles of eggs, clucking, fighting.

Appraisal (detail)

Once in a while, Grant's parents examined his drawings. His father solemnly peered at a hen as though he were judging it at the county fair. "That's a lot of eggs for one hen to lay," was all he said.

Grant's father was very serious. He felt that everything should have a definite purpose. Drawing would never get the crops planted or harvested. Why couldn't Grant be more like his brother, Frank, who was four years older? Frank was so good at tinkering with machinery that he could already fix some of the farm tools.

Grant's mother was more encouraging. She thought his interest in art was just fine, and she admired his talent. She believed that someday he would be famous. But others weren't so sure.

At the one-room schoolhouse he attended, Grant was often daydreaming when Miss Linden, the teacher, called on him. And by mid-morning, he was usually squirming in his desk like the snakes he chased outside. Sometimes Miss Linden just gave up, and told Grant to go outside and keep himself busy for a while. Grant waited for these moments.

Outside, everything was different. Grant sometimes fumbled for answers in geography or arithmetic, but he never missed anything going on around him. Like a sponge, he absorbed even the tiniest details of everything he saw. As he lay in a nearby meadow, he would gaze at the crisp white schoolhouse. In back of it were two neat little outhouses where the boys and girls went to the bathroom. In front was a scraggly young tree. To young Grant, the schoolyard looked like a stage, the way it rose suddenly from surrounding fields of corn. In the distance, the haze on a wooded grove shaped the trees into green balloons. It was the perfect place for a daydream.

Seed Time and Harvest

One day, Grant began to think about "The Midnight Ride of Paul Revere," a poem his mother had read to him a few days earlier. When the United States was struggling for independence from England in the Revolutionary War, Revere saw enemy soldiers approaching. He galloped his horse through the streets of local villages shouting, "The British are coming! The British are coming!"

In Grant's imagination, the story changed to "The Midnight Ride of Grant Wood." He charged into Anamosa, the nearest town, to warn of a cyclone approaching. Everyone hailed him as a hero. He tried his daydream in real life by dashing into the schoolhouse with his awful warning. After Miss Linden saw that there was no cyclone, she rewarded Grant's imagination with a spanking he never forgot.

Midnight Ride of Paul Revere

Grant was as fidgety in church as he was in school. He didn't like sitting still for an hour in a stiff-collared Sunday shirt, listening to the preacher shout about God's punishments for sin. In fact, nobody looked like they were having a very good time. Men's faces drooped as they sweated along with the preacher. They wore starched white shirts, solemn black coats; and sometimes, clean overalls that looked out of place.

The women looked just as grim. Most of them combed their hair back into buns so tight that Grant wondered how they could close their eyes. As they craned their necks and bobbed their heads to gossip, some of the women reminded Grant of his chickens.

No indoor activity held Grant's interest for long. He was much happier roaming around outdoors. Grant loved to explore the countryside to see how many different plants and animals he could find. He sang the names of wildflowers: "Black-eyed Susan, Johnny-jump-up, bouncing Betts . . ." And he was good at spotting birds. In fact, the local newspaper wrote that: "Master Grant Wood, only ten years of age, reports that he has found fifty-five varieties of birds in his neighborhood. His communication on this subject is very interesting and shows that he is an observing, thoughtful, wide-awake boy."

Nothing impressed Grant more than the fields of the Wood family's farm. Since they looked different each week, they became Grant's calendar. Spring was planting time. His father's plow carved huge squares of black earth into the bright green hillsides. He planted corn and oat seed, and in a few weeks, tender green shoots peeked out of the dark furrows. Grant thought the land looked like a giant version of his mother's calico comforters, tied with green yarn. In the heat of July and August the leafy stalks shot up so fast that sometimes the joints made a faint popping sound.

Spring Turning

Dinner for Threshers

But nothing was more exciting than threshing day. Near the end of every summer, all the farmers in the area worked together to help each other harvest oats. One worker operated a steam-powered giant of a threshing machine that separated the oat grains from their stems. Everyone else hauled in wagon-loads of oats to feed the thresher. One by one, each farm's crop was harvested.

Every day Grant heard the noisy thresher working closer and closer to the Wood farm. Finally, it was there, ready to separate his father's oats. As the first sun flooded the farmyard, about a dozen men and older boys from surrounding farms showed up to work. All morning they labored under the broiling

sun, while Grant and his dog, a collie named Dewey, watched the sputtering, oat-eating thresher.

The high point for Grant and the sweating workers came when the whistle shrieked at noon. Everyone trudged to Grant's house for dinner, the big meal of the day. Three tables were pushed together and covered with tablecloths and the family's best china. The Woods were short on chairs, so the piano stool from the parlor and even some boxes and nail kegs were set around the long eating area. Each place was soon filled with a pair of dirty overalls and a sunburned face with slicked-back hair. The men gobbled mountains of fried chicken, ham, mashed potatoes, vegetables, apple pie and chocolate cake.

Tree Planting Group

Almost every day, Grant's life was rich in food and fun. It was only when money matters came up that he realized the Woods might be what some people considered poor. Though his father never talked much about it, Grant knew his father had borrowed a lot of money from a bank to buy the family farm. He had to pay back a certain amount each month. Every time the Woods managed to save some money, something came along to take it away. Dry weather brought a bad harvest. Once an epidemic of cholera killed almost all of the hogs.

One day Grant read a newspaper advertisement about a drawing contest for children. His father, who didn't usually approve of such things, said Grant could enter it. There was one problem. The drawings had to be in black India ink, which Grant didn't have. Grant's father, who had to ride into town for supplies, said that he would buy him some.

When the wagon creaked home the next day, Grant ran out to meet his father. "Did you remember . . . ?" he asked anxiously.

His father's eyes turned down, and he laid his hand on Grant's shoulder. "I'm sorry, son. The smallest bottle of India ink they had was twenty-five cents. We simply can't afford it."

But for the most part, Grant's life was very happy. When he received a box of colored pencils for Christmas one year, he thought he had everything a boy could ever want. His world was a patchwork of hills and fields, dotted with a few trees, animals and farm buildings. Grant wondered if the kings in his father's history books had ever ruled lands as fine as his.

— CHAPTER TWO —

A New Home

In 1900, when Grant was nine years old, his father became very ill. He had always suffered from asthma, which left him short of breath after hard work. But this was different. He gasped for air, and the veins of his forehead bulged in purple cords. A doctor in Anamosa told Grant's father he had suffered a mild heart attack. The doctor warned him to take it easy, or it could happen again. But Grant's father had to raise crops and livestock to feed his family. And soon he went back to work, as hard as ever.

Although the stubborn man didn't listen to the doctor, he could not ignore his body. After a second heart attack, he was too weak to leave the house. "Son," he told Grant, "you're going to have to help Frank as best you can until I'm on my feet again."

It should have been a few more years before Grant had to do so much farm work. But the Woods had no choice. Grant's days of exploring the countryside were over. While their father watched sadly from his hickory rocker, Frank and Grant tried their best to handle all the chores on the farm. The neighbors helped whenever they could spare time from their own farms, but working in the fields, milking twenty cows in the morning and evening, and tending to hogs, sheep and chickens, left Grant too tired to draw.

Grant's father died about nine months after his first heart attack. Grant and Frank struggled through a summer of farming while their mother took care of their younger brother Jack and baby sister Nan. The boys tried their hardest, but they weren't old or strong enough for much of the work.

One day Grant and Frank were hauling cans of their milk into Anamosa when they saw an unfamiliar horse and buggy raising dust in the distance. Frank figured it must be a stranger. Nobody he knew had a horse like that. Grant's eyes popped as the buggy drew closer. It was their grandfather! Grandpa Weaver lived in Cedar Rapids, a city twenty-five miles away, but his visits to the farm were rare. When the boys returned for dinner, they learned why Grandpa had come.

"Your mother tells me you two have been doing a good job of taking care of the farm," their Grandfather began. "We're proud of you. But pretty soon school will be starting, and you won't be able to do all the chores. And your mother says that whatever happens, she is going to see that you go on with your studies."

He went on to explain that with the money owed on the farm, the family could not afford to hire help. He finally got to the point: "How would you like to move to Cedar Rapids?"

Grant and Frank could scarcely believe it. Cedar Rapids was one of Iowa's fastest-growing cities, more than ten times the size of Anamosa. Grant liked the country, but he had heard magical things about Cedar Rapids. The houses had bathrooms with indoor toilets. He would even have friends within walking distance. Grant wanted to move immediately.

He didn't have to wait long. The farm was sold in less than a month, and the family held an auction to sell the farm tools and livestock. It all thrilled Grant, until he realized the family would have to sell their animals. There wouldn't be any room for them in a small yard in Cedar Rapids. Even his beloved dog Dewey had to be given to a neighbor. Grant wondered if he would ever see the farm again. Somehow, it seemed that things would never be the same.

Appraisal

The Woods used money from selling the farm to buy a house in Cedar Rapids. But once again, they had to take a loan from a bank. Grant's mother could make money only by taking in laundry and sewing for people. The little bit she earned had to go a long way.

Still, Grant was happy, especially when he was drawing. In eighth grade, he drew a cluster of oak leaves that won a prize of five dollars in a nationwide contest sponsored by a crayon company.

The problem was, very few other Cedar Rapids boys were interested in art. They wanted to be store owners, or mechanics for the new-fangled automobiles chugging down the streets of the bustling city. Nobody really cared about drawing or painting. Then Grant entered high school and met a boy his age named Marvin Cone. Marvin also loved to draw, paint and build things. Best of all, he would try anything. Grant's shyness melted around the friendly boy.

One day, Grant suggested that they make plaster masks of each other's faces. Marvin agreed, and the boys poured the white goop over themselves. They breathed—or tried to breathe—through straws stuck in their mouths. But the straws collapsed, and the boys nearly suffocated. They ripped at their masks, which had now dried on their faces. "Youch!" hollered Grant, as a chunk of his hair pulled off with the plaster.

In order to keep drawing Grant needed art supplies, so he decided to try to sell one of his paintings, a tree-lined bluff overlooking a river.

"How much do you think the painting is worth?" a woman asked him.

"It isn't worth much," Grant softly replied, looking at his feet. "But I need eight dollars." To his surprise, he got his asking price. Before long, other adults in Cedar Rapids began to buy some of his artwork.

Grant used part of his earnings to buy a monthly art magazine called the *Craftsman,* which ran an instructional column each month by a well-known designer named Ernest Batchelder. Grant studied the lessons carefully, and waited eagerly for each new issue of the magazine. He bought all the supplies Batchelder suggested: a drawing board, papers for drawing and painting, large and small brushes, watercolors and India ink.

Grant drew in crisp, solid lines and shapes, with hills that billowed like his mother's quilts on the clothesline. This was the style of art Batchelder encouraged in his articles. To Grant it was perfect for the rolling countryside and sturdy-looking people he saw around him.

His high school art teacher didn't agree. The teacher favored a new style, called Impressionism, that blurred objects, as though they were being seen in a dream. To show Grant the technique, the teacher took one of Grant's best watercolor landscapes over to the sink, and held it under running water that smeared his clean lines together. Grant was shocked, but still determined to paint his way.

On high school graduation night, Grant surprised everyone with his cheerfulness. The shy boy usually hated to be in the spotlight, even if it was for a few seconds to accept his diploma. But Grant was smiling, and puffed up as tall as his short body could rise. Grant wasn't excited about graduation, but about what would happen afterward. He wanted to attend the Handicraft Guild in Minneapolis, a well-known art school.

That night Grant climbed aboard a train headed for Minneapolis. As the train rumbled out of the station, Grant had nothing but thirty dollars and some high hopes. He didn't know whether the Handicraft Guild would accept him as a student, or whether he could even afford the classes. But he knew he had to try.

CHAPTER THREE

Studying Art

Sketch for *Fall Plowing*

Grant was in luck. The director of the Handicraft Guild was impressed with Grant's determination. He enrolled Grant and helped him find work to pay his tuition. Grant stretched painting canvas over frames and cleaned the Guild's studio. To save money, he even moved out of the room where he lived and slept on a bench in a park. When it rained, he sipped coffee in a restaurant that stayed open all night.

It was worth it. Grant got to study under his idol, Ernest Batchelder, the designer whose articles Grant had studied through high school. Grant liked Batchelder even better in person. Batchelder's favorite artists weren't the Impressionists that Grant's high school teacher crowed about, but painters who lived almost five hundred years earlier. These Renaissance painters, as they were called, filled their work with clear details. Each painting told a story. Many pictured stories from the Bible, or from ancient Greek and Roman myths. These artists sometimes took many years to finish a painting, Batchelder explained. They applied colors slowly and precisely, leaving nothing to chance. To Grant, they were just the opposite of painters who intentionally blurred their subjects. He would later say that his summer at the Handicraft Guild was the most valuable art training he ever received.

Fall Plowing

Grant Wood with his painting *Arbor Day*

When the summer ended, Grant returned to Iowa to teach art at a one-room country school much like the one he attended as a boy. Three nights a week he took a 28-mile train trip to attend art classes at the University of Iowa. He was still nearly broke, so he just walked in the first night of classes and started painting at an easel. If anyone knew that he hadn't paid to enroll, they never did anything about it.

Grant thought it would be funny if he became the best painter at the university, and never paid a cent for tuition. But he didn't get famous in that class. In fact, he didn't seem to make much of an impression at all. Grant felt discouraged. Even though he was now a much better painter, his art had received more compliments from his friends back in high school.

"Maybe I should go to a bigger city, or try a different school," he wondered. Some of his relatives thought differently. They felt that Grant should forget this art "nonsense" and get a steady job. But when people criticized Grant, his mother insisted that he would someday be a great artist.

Grant moved to Chicago, where he got a job designing and making silver jewelry. Soon he saved enough money to pay for night classes at Chicago's Art Institute. Perhaps, he thought, he was finally on the right track. Grant felt so assured by his new success that he and another designer left the large silversmith shop where they worked. The two young men started their own business making silver jewelry. They were fine craftsmen, but terrible businessmen. Especially Grant. He wanted every piece to be absolutely perfect, and worked too slowly to make much money. After eighteen months, they had to close shop. Once again, Grant was flat broke. He had to borrow train fare just to return to Cedar Rapids.

Grant peered glumly out the window as the train rolled through the farmland he knew so well. He had hoped to come home a famous artist, and make his mother proud.

Fertility

Now, he worried, she and all the others would consider him a big failure. But Grant's mother had bigger problems. She could no longer pay the mortgage on the Woods' house, and the bank was taking it away. There was nothing Grant could do. He was down to his last dollar.

Grant put that dollar to good use. It was all he needed to make a deposit for a patch of wooded land near Indian Creek, just outside Cedar Rapids. "I can do the rest," he told his mother.

Like his father many years earlier, Grant quickly built a small cabin on his land. He put in a vegetable garden that was soon growing enough to feed them. Grant's mother added to the dinner table by picking wild blackberries, dandelion greens, and other foods in the woods. By now Grant's older brother Frank had opened an automobile parts business in another town. His younger brother Jack was a mechanic who wasn't interested in a cabin in the woods. His sister Nan was still in high school in Cedar Rapids. She lived in town with Grant's aunt, but enjoyed visiting the cabin.

Wood's cottage near Indian Creek in Cedar Rapids, 1916

The small, unheated cabin was fine for the summer. But Grant knew that as the temperature cooled, he would need a warmer home. An old friend named Paul Hanson had an idea. He had bought two pieces of land nearby and offered one to Grant in exchange for help in building a house in each yard.

Grant worked very slowly and carefully, just like he did at his silversmith shop, to make sure everything was perfect. His friend Paul was afraid they would never finish the houses before winter.

As Paul feared, when the first snow fell in November, the houses were not ready. Paul and his wife moved into town for the winter, but Grant and his mother had nowhere to go. They moved into a shack owned by Paul. It was small, but it had a wood stove to fight the winter cold. Some days, the temperature dropped to twenty degrees below zero, and the Woods huddled under heavy comforters. But Grant kept their spirits up, especially at Christmas time.

January

Grant announced that since it was Christmas, they should feast on a duck dinner. It didn't matter that all the Woods could afford was a piece of round steak. Grant wrapped the meat around a stick and covered it with cloth. Then, with the same careful attention he gave to making a silver bracelet or shingling a roof, he carved an elaborate duck head on the end of the stick!

It was like Grant to spend his time on something that was fun, but not profitable. Several people in Cedar Rapids admired his artistic skills, and he might have made money painting their portraits or decorating their houses. The problem wasn't that he was lazy, Grant just never actively looked for work. Once he stayed up all night decorating a wagon for a young girl to use in a parade. Another time he made three-foot concrete "giant" footprints leading to his cottage. But Grant wasn't making a living like his brothers. Sometimes he even wondered to himself: What was he going to do?

That question was answered within a year, when the United States entered World War I. All young men Grant's age were required to serve as soldiers, and he was sent to a training camp. He became very popular because he sketched portraits of the other soldiers in his company.

Grant never went to battle because he became very ill. When he recovered, he was sent to Washington, D.C. There, as a camouflage artist, Grant painted cannons and wagons in color patterns that would blend in with the woods, so they would not be seen by the enemy. He liked the job, but it didn't last long. In less than a year, the war was over.

Grant came home on Christmas Eve, 1918. His mother, his sister Nan, and others welcomed him back to Cedar Rapids, but he was a little confused. He asked himself: "What now?"

Parson Weems' Fable

CHAPTER FOUR

Struggling for a Style

Grant's cousin was a metalworker and an amateur artist himself. He knew and respected Grant's talent. He also knew Fan Prescott, the principal of Jackson Junior High in Cedar Rapids. He hoped he could convince Miss Prescott to hire Grant as an art teacher.

Miss Prescott had her doubts. Grant was getting a reputation in Cedar Rapids for being unpredictable. He was now twenty-eight years old. Most of his friends had worked for years, had married, and were raising families. During this same period, Grant rarely even had a steady job.

Miss Prescott's suspicions grew when she met Grant face to face. Because he owned hardly anything else, Grant showed up for the meeting in his stiff wool army uniform. He was so nervous, he couldn't look Miss Prescott in the eye. As he spoke, he swayed slowly back and forth on his feet, like the pendulum of an old grandfather clock.

Cartoon for *Parson Weems' Fable*

But Miss Prescott also believed in hunches, and she had one about Grant. She felt that beneath his shy, awkward manner, he was a very creative person.

If Grant could interest her students in art, she didn't care if he wore his army boots to class. Miss Prescott gave him a job and said she would let Grant teach his way. But if he couldn't get results from the students, he would be fired.

Miss Prescott kept her word. Even when Grant showed up for the first day of class in his army boots, or when she walked past Grant's classroom one day and heard him lecturing on how to catch rabbits, she kept her mouth shut. Her hunch proved correct. Even though Grant had no lesson plans, he knew how to make art fun and interesting for every student.

Once, one of the rowdiest boys refused to draw a group of flowers Grant had put in a vase.

"That's sissy stuff!" the student sneered.

"What is something that isn't sissy stuff?" Grant asked.

"An airplane," the boy said.

"Then draw an airplane," Grant suggested. He urged students to use their imaginations, even in the school cafeteria. Potatoes became "the succulent seed-vessels of the magical mingo tree." Boiled cabbage was transformed into "the crisp and tender leaf of the Clishy-Clashy vine." Grant became so good at entertaining his students that other children brought to the principal's office for misbehaving were often told to "Go to Mr. Wood's class for awhile."

Grant was drawing attention to not only his teaching, but his artwork. His paintings were exhibited for the first time in a Cedar Rapids department store. Another artist was also featured—Grant's high school friend, Marvin Cone. Grant and Marvin talked a lot about art, just like they did when they were younger.

One day in 1920 Grant suggested that the two of them go to Paris for the summer. Paris was still considered the center of the art world, just like it had been when Grant was younger. Very few American artists—especially ones from Cedar Rapids, Iowa—were taken seriously unless they had studied in Paris. Marvin agreed.

As soon as school ended for the summer, the two young men took a steamship to Paris. They didn't have enough money to enroll in art school, so they just set up their easels on the streets and began painting. Often, they worked elbow-to-elbow with other people doing the same thing. On rainy days, they studied paintings in the Louvre, one of the world's finest art museums.

When Grant returned in the fall, he was able to do more than just teach. He received phone calls from wealthy people: "Mr. Wood, I am decorating my home, and I understand you've worked in *Paris*. Would you be able to help me?"

Miss Prescott continued to be impressed with Grant's teaching. When she became principal at McKinley High School, she insisted that Grant come with her as art teacher. Not everyone shared her enthusiasm for the offbeat instructor. One school board member complained that Grant was often late to class.

"Grant Wood is more valuable to me arriving at half-past ten than many teachers are at seven o'clock in the morning!" Miss Prescott shot back. As usual, the fiery principal got her way. Grant never forgot her support.

"If I ever become famous," he said, "there will be only two people who won't be surprised . . . my mother and Fan Prescott."

Grant's style appealed to the people of Cedar Rapids. But Grant was frustrated that he was still unknown as an artist outside his city. He decided that nobody would pay any attention to an artist from Iowa, and that he should return to Paris to study.

Miss Prescott allowed Grant a year of absence from his job, and he crossed the ocean again. This time he had saved some money, so he enrolled in a popular Paris art school called Julian's Academy. All the other students were either from France or could speak the French language. But not Grant, so he

kept to himself and painted. The other students nicknamed him "Tête de bois"—"Woodenhead."

Grant learned that the impressionistic style his high school teacher had once hailed as "modern" was now considered old fashioned. The latest rage was abstract art. Abstract artists attacked their canvases with big brushes, or even threw the paint at the canvas. They often worked very quickly, unlike Grant's slower, precise technique.

At the end of the school year at Julian's, several students took a painting vacation in the countrysides of France and Italy. Grant set up his easel in many places only to find paint stains where other artists had wiped their brushes on a fence, or splattered colors on the ground. He wondered how many people had already painted the same scene.

Still, Grant kept painting. He sold enough of his work along the way to pay the cost of his travels. In fact, his art was far more popular with the local people in France and Italy than was the abstract work of his companions. Grant only wished the art critics liked his work as much as ordinary people did.

Grant wasn't famous when he returned to Cedar Rapids in the fall, but he was among friends. His old teaching job was waiting for him, and more local people than ever bought his work. One of his best patrons was a funeral home owner named David Turner.

Even though Turner was a busy man, he always found time to help Grant. He drove him to appointments when the artist's car broke down. He even found work for Grant decorating other funeral homes. One day he approached Grant with his best offer yet.

"I have an old carriage house above my garage," Turner said. "It needs a little fixing up, but it has steam heat. It could be the perfect artist's studio. I won't charge you any rent."

Grant soon moved in, and as always, his mother moved with him. He had always lived with her, except when he was abroad. Since nobody had lived in the carriage house for years, he needed an address so he could receive mail. Thinking of his patron, his studio became Number 5 Turner Alley.

As usual, he had fun decorating his new home. To give the doors of a bookcase an antique look, he stretched old overalls over them, smeared them with plaster, then painted them bronze. He covered the floor with 4-inch squares of wood in a checkerboard pattern. "Now all you need are giant checkers," a friend joked. So he made some checkers, as big as saucers.

Grant painted a big clock on the front door, and attached a metal arrow that could be moved to any position. Above the clock read: "Grant Wood Will Return to the Studio At—," and the arrow pointed to the time Grant would be back. The arrow could also point to sentences such as "Is giving a party" or "Is taking a bath."

Grant also thought up clever ideas for other people's homes. Soon, he was making more money as an interior decorator than as a painter. The problem was, he worked very slowly. Home-owners had to put up with rooms that were left in a shambles for months. Tactfully, they would approve his work and ask when he would be finished.

Grant often replied that something wasn't quite right. He needed to alter things just a bit, and it wouldn't take much longer. But it always did. Whether he was decorating, painting, or anything else, his work seemed to take forever. He thought of the Renaissance artists he admired so much. They took all the time they needed, and nobody seemed to mind. He began to wish he had been born five hundred years ago.

In 1926, Grant made a third trip to Paris, this time to try to modernize his technique. He didn't impress the modern art world in France much more than before. But he did bring home a new painting style that set tongues buzzing in Cedar Rapids. Grant explained that he was going to become an abstract artist.

He listened to some music and painted what he heard in wild circles and slashes across the canvas. Grant enjoyed trying something different, but his friends said it looked awful. He began applying paint with a knife instead of a paintbrush, but the results weren't any better.

Fortunately, he soon won an art assignment that gave him no time for knives and paint splatters. A large new memorial coliseum honoring soldiers who had fought in World War I was being built in Cedar Rapids. Grant, now a well-known artist in his community, was hired to design and supervise the building of a huge stained-glass window at one end of the coliseum. Grant quit his teaching job to devote all his time to the project.

Grant decided to have the window made in Germany, home of the world's best stained-glass makers. Some people in Cedar Rapids howled in protest.

How could Grant possibly insult the brave soldiers by making their window in Germany—the nation's enemy in World War I—they huffed. It didn't matter that Americans and Germans were now at peace, or that Grant was simply looking for the best craftsmen available. When the beautiful window was installed in the coliseum, most people could only complain that it was made in Germany. An elaborate ceremony had been planned to welcome the work of stained glass, but it was canceled in protest.

Grant felt like they were breaking the window over his head. This was his largest art project ever, and almost everyone criticized him. It would have been a total disaster, except for one thing.

When he was in Germany, Grant strolled through an art museum one day. Some old paintings seemed to jump off the wall at him. The faces were full of

Veteran's Memorial Building Window

emotion. The scenery was rich in detail. There was no crazy splattering of paint like in abstract art, or fuzzy shapes like those the Impressionists created. These careful artists showed exactly what was going on in their work.

They painted in a style called Gothic, which had been popular among European artists more than five hundred years earlier. As he gazed at the old canvases, he realized this was how he had always wanted his art to look. All the way home, Grant wondered how he could apply the rich style of the Gothic artists to his own painting.

When he opened the door to his studio back in Cedar Rapids, he found his answer. As always, his mother was there to greet him. But this time, he saw her kind, seventy-year-old face in a different way. The lines around her bright eyes were like roads leading back to the old family farm.

Grant's head flooded with memories of that wonderful period of his life. Like a wave, the rolling, dreamy landscape swelled before him once again. So did the livestock, especially his favorite Plymouth Rock hens. The faces of the country people passed before him: the hard-working, serious farmers like his father, even the gossipy ladies at church.

Grant asked himself why he had been painting the French countryside and Italian villages while ignoring the people and things he'd known all his life. Maybe the rest of the art world revolved around places like Paris. But from now on, he would focus on the Iowa land and people he knew best.

— CHAPTER FIVE —

Success at Last

Since his mother's face had inspired Grant to paint what he knew best, he decided she should be one of his first subjects. Although her health was growing poor, she agreed to pose for him. After all, she was the one who had always thought he would become a famous artist.

Like the Gothic painters he admired, Grant worked more slowly and carefully than ever before. He used small brushes and applied many coats of paint. He added depth with several layers of clear varnish, which he smoothed with a razor blade.

The result was a painting he called *Woman with Plants,* and it won a prize at the Iowa State Fair. It was also shown in an exhibition at Chicago's Art Institute, where Grant had once taken art lessons. Though it drew little attention there, Grant didn't get discouraged. Something inside told him he was moving in the right direction.

Next he decided to paint a landscape. He chose a hilly little village called Stone City, very close to where he grew up. When Grant was a boy, it was a bustling town full of stonecutters who chiseled limestone blocks out of the hillside for buildings and bridges. Now other building materials were used more often, and Stone City was almost empty.

Grant wanted people to understand his subjects, but he didn't want to merely paint an exact copy of the village. "Anyone can get that just by taking a picture," he pointed out. No, it would have to be different.

He recalled the way he had viewed the country when he was a boy. The hills seemed fatter, the roads curvier. Trees had a round, puffy shape like

Stone City, Iowa

grapes or blackberries. That was the way he painted *Stone City*. It looked real—and not quite real—at the same time.

When the painting was first displayed at the 1930 Iowa State Fair, Grant noticed a farmer inspecting its roller coaster hills. The farmer backed away and shook his head. "I wouldn't give thirty-five cents an acre for that land!" he frowned.

But most people liked it. *Stone City* won the top prize for landscapes at the state fair. Grant was beginning to be regarded as the finest painter in the state.

By now, Grant regularly searched the countryside for new ideas to paint. On one of these "scouting trips," Grant noticed a funny little farmhouse with a large, bullet-shaped Gothic window. This was the type of window used in the huge churches of Europe that were made by craftsmen who lived at the same time as the Gothic artists he admired. The thought of the plain Iowa country house imitating the soaring cathedrals made him laugh.

"I guess this is an American Gothic," he chuckled.

That house became the background for his next painting. His idea was to place a farm woman and man in front of it. As usual, he wanted to paint faces he knew well. He asked his sister Nan to pose as the woman. For the farmer, Grant asked his dentist, Dr. McKeeby, to pose.

As with *Stone City,* Grant did not paint Nan and Dr. McKeeby exactly as they looked. He stretched their faces and necks, as though the summer heat were beginning to melt them. They looked as rigid and serious as the people who sat in church when Grant was a boy. But they also looked like they could endure the hardships of farm life, such as droughts and cyclones.

In 1930, both *Stone City* and *American Gothic* were shown at the Chicago exhibition where the year before *Woman with Plants* had received little attention. This time was different. *American Gothic* won a prize and was bought by the Art Institute for three hundred dollars.

More important, it caused a sensation with the public. It quickly drew the biggest crowds of any artwork in the museum. The painting was sent to other museums for display, and was just as popular. When *American Gothic* was shipped to London, people crowded around the painting as if it were a movie star.

Most art critics praised *American Gothic* and *Stone City*. Here, they proclaimed, was an American artist who painted American subjects in an original, *American* way. Grant proved you didn't have to live in Paris, or even in an American art center such as New York, to be a great artist. Iowa, often considered the home of "hicks" by those in the big cities, had produced a world-class artist in overalls.

Grant's sister, Nan Wood Graham, and dentist, Dr. B. H. McKeeby

After thirty-nine years of being largely unknown, Grant was suddenly a superstar of the art world. Never had an American artist become so popular so quickly. And rarely had one been less prepared for fame. In many ways, Grant was still the shy boy who mumbled and could not look strangers in the eye. He felt awkward when newspapers and magazines interviewed him. He was uncomfortable at fancy receptions honoring his work. He felt best when he was painting. So he put on his overalls and went to work.

Portrait of Nan

Filled with new confidence, Grant once again looked to his boyhood memories for ideas. The *Midnight Ride of Paul Revere* grew out of the poem his mother had once read to him. *Arbor Day* celebrated the annual holiday when Grant and his classmates planted a tree in the bare schoolyard. In *Dinner for Threshers,* he cut away the side of a farmhouse so a scene from that big day looked as if it were happening in a dollhouse. And his favorite Plymouth Rock chickens managed to find their way into many paintings, including *Appraisal* and *Adolescence.*

The gossipy ladies at his old church showed up in a painting called *Daughters of Revolution*. Grant used them to show the meanness and prejudice of some people he had known. He was especially thinking of the ones who hated the window he had designed for the Cedar Rapids coliseum because it was made in Germany.

Grant's paintings made most people smile, and some people angry. It was hard to look at his art without feeling *something*. Many people now talked or wrote to him. Even the pope of the Catholic Church wanted to know more about his work.

All this new support helped him overcome his shyness. He began to tell people his feelings about art. "I want to reach everyday people, not just the artists and art critics of the world," he explained. He talked about his years of trying to paint subjects from foreign lands, in other artists' styles, and about how he finally began painting the things he knew best, in the way he felt most comfortable.

To Grant's surprise, a new style of painting was named after *his* work. It was called Regionalism, because most of Grant's subjects were from the same region in Iowa. Other American painters who concentrated on certain areas of the country also became very popular. Suddenly, an artist didn't have to be from Europe to be respected.

But it wasn't enough for Grant. Ever since he had taught boys and girls in Cedar Rapids, Grant had always helped others develop their art skills. It bothered Grant that the most respected places for promising artists to develop their skills were either in Europe or in a few art colonies on the east coast of the United States. These places, where people lived among artists and painted every day, were too far away and expensive for most students in the Midwest. Grant decided to start an affordable art colony in Iowa, designed for aspiring young midwestern artists.

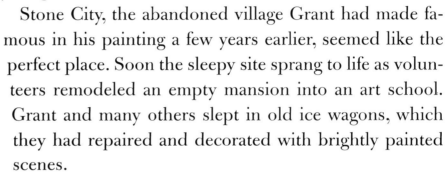

Stone City, the abandoned village Grant had made famous in his painting a few years earlier, seemed like the perfect place. Soon the sleepy site sprang to life as volunteers remodeled an empty mansion into an art school. Grant and many others slept in old ice wagons, which they had repaired and decorated with brightly painted scenes.

There had never been an art school quite like Stone City. There was no sitting around in studios here. Students painted outdoors and got closer to barnyard animals than most of them had ever been. Chickens sometimes pecked at ribbons of oil paint squeezed out of tubes, thinking they were worms. Occasionally a person painting in a pasture would have to outrun a bull that didn't like visitors!

Grant remembered his classmates in Paris who snubbed the everyday people in their work. He wanted to open his art colony to the public, so everyone could see what they were doing. Each Sunday they held a giant open house, where people visited the art colony while they munched a hot dog and bought paintings offered by the students. Sometimes a thousand people jammed into the little village.

But Stone City ran into problems. Grant had launched it during the depression, one of the hardest financial times in American history. Close to half the students were given scholarships for their instruction and meals, or received them free in return for doing chores at the art colony. Stone City was deep in debt, and Grant had to close it.

Even then, Grant didn't quit teaching. He accepted a job at the University of Iowa, where he had sneaked into an art class many years earlier. Although he was now a famous artist, many professors disliked him. Some felt that because he had hardly any formal training, he had no right to be teaching at a college.

They also didn't think he behaved much like a professor. He still wore his overalls most of the time and didn't act very serious in the classroom. Once, he came into class rolling an operating table he had borrowed from the university's medical school. It was piled high with paintings from his students. "Today," he announced with a grin, "we will operate on your artwork." He even held a free Saturday afternoon workshop for people not in his art classes. Everyone from children to farm housewives brought in their drawings or paintings for Grant's suggestions.

Though some professors didn't like his habits, Grant Wood had become the most famous artist in the United States. He awakened millions of Americans to the talents of their local artists. He helped people see beauty in their own backyards and everyday lives. In the end, it didn't matter that Grant was shy or that he came from a farm and had little art schooling. "The best ideas I ever had came to me while milking a cow," he told people.

Unfortunately, many of those ideas were never put on canvas. In 1942, twelve years after he painted *American Gothic* and fifty-one years after he was born, Grant died of cancer.

Shortly after his death, Regionalism, the painting style he created, declined.

But then, thirty years after *American Gothic* was painted, a new generation was drawn to the faces of the country people who peered from the canvas. The famous faces were often used in magazines, even in movies. People thought they were the perfect image of determined, hard-working "middle-class" Americans.

As time went on, advertisers took advantage of *American Gothic*'s popularity. The country couple was used to sell everything from corn flakes to color televisions.

They were also used in funny ways. The heads of the original pair were replaced with famous people such as presidents and their wives. Sometimes the people Grant painted were placed in a new setting, such as a beach party.

Today *American Gothic* is one of the most famous paintings ever created. It is art for everybody, just like the quiet artist in overalls wanted.

Drawing and Painting like Grant Wood

When Grant Wood began to draw he used the materials available to him: charred black sticks pulled from the cooking stove and white cardboard torn from cracker boxes. He drew what he liked best — chickens. Starting with simple egg shapes, he drew the basic structure of the chicken, adding the beak and legs with rough lines.

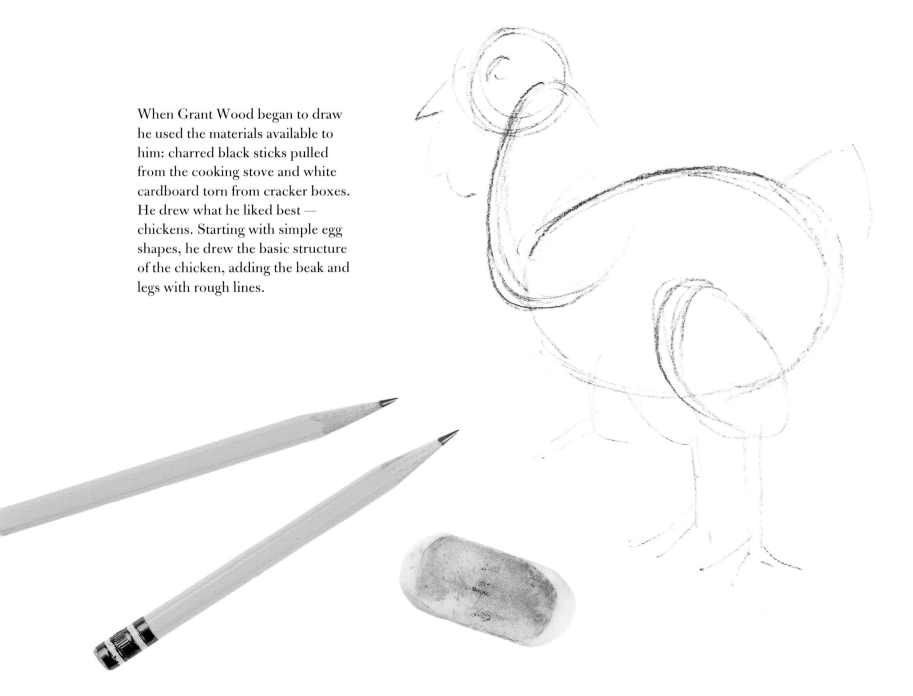

Once Grant understood the basic shape of the chicken, he continued adding details. From these loose sketches, a clearer picture would begin to appear.

Finally, Grant set out to refine his loose drawing. The chicken took shape as Grant added contour, shading and fine detail. For example, feathers emerged from what were once just squiggles.

As he acquired more tools, such as colored pencils, brushes and water-colors, Grant was able to bring his drawings to life by adding color. He picked his colors carefully and slowly labored over each detail just like the Renaissance painters he had grown to admire. Color was applied, then blended with an eraser or added layer upon layer to deepen the colors. Once finished, Grant's work had a lifelike quality.

Even though pencils, paints and paper are readily available today, fancy art supplies aren't necessary to learn to draw well. Like Grant, start drawing with simple shapes and add details later. With only basic tools and some practice, you can learn to draw and paint like Grant Wood.

Grant Wood's artwork can be found in museums and private collections throughout the world. The paintings in this book can be found at the following locations:

Page 6
Detail of page 21

Page 9
Seed Time and Harvest, 1937
Lithograph, edition of 250, 7½ × 12¼ in.
Courtesy Associated American Artists, New York

Page 10
Midnight Ride of Paul Revere, 1931
Oil on composition board, 30 × 40 in.
The Metropolitan Museum of Art,
Arthur Hoppock Hearn Fund, 1950 (50.117).
© 1988 The Metropolican Museum of Art

Pages 12–13
Spring Turning, 1936
Oil on Masonite, 18⅛ × 40 in.
Reynolda House Museum of American Art,
Winston-Salem, North Carolina

Pages 14–15
Dinner for Threshers, 1934
Oil on hardboard, 19½ × 79½ in.
The Fine Arts Museums of San Francisco,
gift of Mr. and Mrs. John D. Rockefeller 3rd

Page 16
Tree Planting Group, 1937
Lithograph, edition of 250, 8⅜ × 10⅞ in.
Courtesy Associated American Artists, New York

Page 18
Spring in Town, 1941
Oil on Masonite, 26 × 24½ in.
The Sheldon Swope Art Gallery, Terre Haute,
Indiana

Page 21
Appraisal, 1931
Oil on composition board, 29½ × 35¼ in.
Carnegie-Stout Public Library, Dubuque, Iowa

Page 24
Fall Plowing (sketch), 1931
Oil on Masonite, 17⅞ × 19⅞ in.
Davenport Museum of Art, Davenport, Iowa

Page 25
Fall Plowing, 1931
Oil on canvas, 30 × 40¾ in.
Deere & Company Art Collection

Page 26
Grant Wood with *Arbor Day,* 1932, in his
studio at No. 5 Turner Alley, Cedar Rapids
Photograph by John W. Barry
Cedar Rapids Museum of Art Archives, gift of
John B. Turner II in memory of Happy Young
Turner. © Cedar Rapids Museum of Art

Page 28
Fertility, 1939
Lithograph, edition of 250, 8⅞ × 11⅞ in.
Courtesy Associated American Artists, New York

Page 29
Grant Wood built this rustic cottage near Indian
Creek in Cedar Rapids, Iowa. In 1916 it served as
an interim home for his family after his mother had
to give up her home in Cedar Rapids.
Cedar Rapids Museum of Art Archives, gift of
John B. Turner II in memory of Happy Young
Turner. © Cedar Rapids Museum of Art

Page 30
January, 1940
Oil on Masonite, 18 × 24 in.
Collection of Arthur E. Imperatore

Page 32
Parson Weems' Fable, 1939
Oil on canvas, 38⅜ × 50⅛ in.
Amon Carter Museum, Fort Worth, Texas

Page 33
Parson Weems' Fable (cartoon), 1939
Charcoal, pencil, and chalk on paper, 38⅜ × 50 in.
Private Collection

Page 36
Self-Portrait, 1932
Oil on Masonite, 21 × 18½ in.
Davenport Museum of Art, Davenport, Iowa

Page 40
Veteran's Memorial Building Window, 1929
Stained glass
Veteran's Memorial Commission, City of Cedar
Rapids, Iowa

Page 42
Woman with Plants, 1929
Oil on upsom board, 20½ × 17⅞ in.
Cedar Rapids Museum of Art, Art Association
Purchase. © Cedar Rapids Museum of Art

Page 44
Stone City, Iowa, 1930
Oil on composition board, 30¼ × 40 in.
Joslyn Art Museum, Omaha, Nebraska

Page 46
Nan Wood Graham and Dr. B. H. McKeeby
(detail) at the Art Institute of Chicago, 1942
Cedar Rapids Museum of Art Archives, gift of
John B. Turner II in memory of Happy Young
Turner. © Cedar Rapids Museum of Art

Page 47
American Gothic, 1930
Oil on beaver board, 29½ × 24½ in.
The Art Institute of Chicago, Friends of American
Arts Collection, © 1995 The Art Institute of
Chicago / VAGA, New York, NY

Page 48
Portrait of Nan, 1933
Oil on Masonite, 40 × 30 in.
Elvehjem Museum of Art, University of Wisconsin-
Madison, anonymous loan

To Iowans everywhere

First paperback edition published in 2005 by
Chronicle Books LLC.

Book design by John Hubbard.
Manufactured in Hong Kong.
ISBN 0-8118-4908-2

The Library of Congress has catalogued the
hardcover edition as follows:
    Grant Wood: artist in overalls / John Duggleby.
        p. cm.
    Summary: Follows the life of the Iowa farm boy
who struggled to realize his talents and who painted
in Paris but returned home to focus on the land and
people he knew best.
    ISBN 0-8118-1242-1
    1. Wood, Grant, 1891-1942—Juvenile
literature. 2. Painters—United States—
Biography—Juvenile literature. [1. Wood, Grant,
1891-1942. 2. Artists.] I. Title.
ND237.W795D84   1996
759.13–dc20
95-34070
[B]

Front cover: *Boy Milking Cow*, 1932; Part 1 of
Fruits of Iowa, a 7-part mural; oil on canvas glued to
panels, 45 ½ x 39 ½ in.; Coe College Permanent
Collection of Art, Cedar Rapids, Iowa.

Back cover and frontispiece: *American Gothic*, 1930;
oil on beaver board, 29 ½ x 24 ½ in.; The Art Institute
of Chicago, Friends of American Art Collection;
Photo © 1994 The Art Institute of Chicago,
all rights reserved.

Distributed in Canada by Raincoast Books
9050 Shaughnessy Street
Vancouver, British Columbia V6P 6E5

10 9 8 7 6 5 4 3 2 1

Chronicle Books LLC
85 Second Street
San Francisco, California 94105

www.chroniclekids.com

John Duggleby was born and raised in eastern Iowa, near the areas where Grant Wood lived and painted, and he studied Journalism at the University of Iowa, where Grant Wood taught. He now lives with his daughter, Katie, amid similar rolling hills in McFarland, Wisconsin. *Artist in Overalls: The Life of Grant Wood* is his fifth book for children.

ALSO BY JOHN DUGGLEBY:

Story Painter: The Life of Jacob Lawrence

A Smithsonian Notable Book for Children
A Carter G. Woodson Book Award Recipient

"A visually striking, well-researched biography." —*Horn Book*